WRITING INTERACTIVE FICTION

by
DM Potter

Published by:
The Fairytale Factory Ltd.
Wellington, New Zealand.
All rights reserved.
Copyright DM Potter © 2016

ISBN-13: 978-1539501152
ISBN-10: 1539501159

WRITING INTERACTIVE FICTION

Content

Content (continued)

What is interactive fiction?

In the unlikely event you've picked up this eBook not knowing what interactive fiction is, let's catch you up.

Interactive fiction is the broad description for stories that offer the reader a chance to 'interact' with the story. Readers commonly interact by responding to choices that influence the outcome of the story. Because choices are an integral part of the experience, there are multiple parallel stories throughout an interactive book.

Instead of being on a highway going in one direction (a traditional novel), readers are traversing a network of streets, across different landscapes. The reader experience is exploratory. Each intersection (choice) takes them along a different route (story path or thread). Whereas a novel is linear in structure, middle grade interactive fiction generally has a branching structure. Because choices lead to different story experiences, there are usually multiple endings. Occasionally, multiple paths will lead to only one or a limited set of endings.

Adult interactive fiction tends to experiment with non-traditional forms more than children's interactive fiction. This book concentrates on writing for young people but much of what is discussed is useful and relevant for stories targeted to older readers.

In praise of interactive fiction for kids

Do you remember that first really exciting book when you'd just started reading?

I remember discovering Eric Carle's *The Very Hungry Caterpillar* in the school library when I was about five years old. I have an image of my fingers wiggling through the holes in the pages. I was delighted by it. I made my way through the book – sounding out the words while the pictures helped me. I loved the images of all the food. The very hungry caterpillar and I were at an exotic dinner party. I even remember turning the last page and having my suspicions turn out to be right. There he was! A beautiful butterfly.

The book was hard for me to read, I didn't understand all the words, but I kept going because I was so involved.

I think of *The Very Hungry Caterpillar* as the first interactive book I ever read. It invited me to participate in an exciting way.

Good interactive fiction delivers involvement and delight.

Most people understand that reading fiction is a pleasantly voyeuristic experience. The reader experiences danger, drama and a different world, without having to get out of their comfort zone. This kind of experience is hugely informative for children. From talking to my readers, their teachers, and parents, I understand that reading interactive fiction has the capacity to build empathy and encourages problem solving skills.

Interactive fiction for kids is generally told in second person. You are the main character. You have the adventures. I provide tips about writing in second person in another section (see page 23).

Second person breaks down barriers of gender, race and class. There has been some great diversity in fiction written for kids in the last twenty years, but I like to think interactive fiction was a trailblazer.

A boy came up to me at my first classroom visit to explain how excited he was that the book was 'about me'. "I don't have a normal book family," he said, explaining how he lived in two houses with different siblings in each. "And I still fit in your book!" I liked how he said he didn't have a 'normal book family' rather than that his family wasn't normal.

Up until meeting him, I hadn't heard firsthand how powerful it can feel to fit into a book and what a positive experience that can be. While readers might not know the technical term for second person they do recognize the highly personal experience it can produce.

Teachers have told me that interactive books can often act as a gateway to other books for kids who haven't quite clicked with reading.

Interactive fiction can be completely gender inclusive. In the unlikely event that you don't understand how great this is, here's a joke I read on Twitter last night that may help explain:

> "I'm not hung up on the term 'spacewoman' because I know
> it refers to both women & men." Tim, age 44, male
> spacewoman.
> Tweeted by manwhohasitall

A lot of traditional kids' literature delivers insipid girl characters. Girls get super powers like invisibility so they can hide well, or smarts that keep them in the back seat. Boys get super powers like strength and speed, qualities that allow them to take the lead. Interactive fiction puts an end to the stereotypes because YOU, whoever you are, are the lead character.

I've heard that publishers have a tendency to favor books with male protagonists because girls will still read them, whereas books with female protagonists 'are only for girls' and therefore restrict the size of the potential market. Believe me, girls notice gender stereotyping, and they always have. I certainly did as a child. Girls tell me they love taking charge and driving the story in a *You Say Which Way* adventure.

With second person interactive fiction, *everybody* fits in the story.

Diego Arandojo read a lot of interactive fiction growing up in Argentina. He considers the books to have been "a school" for him. The reason I know about him is that he wrote a musical referencing his favorite titles. You can find out a little bit more about Diego in the reference section (see page 81). (It contains external links so it's probably best explored when you're reading from a tablet or PC and have good internet access.)

The last reason interactive fiction is fantastic is because an author can tell fantastic stories – interactive stories that are richly satisfying, intriguing, exciting, humorous, and imaginative.

In the next section, we'll look at the mechanics of interactive fiction writing.

Writing interactive fiction

STORY

Here's something important to put at the top of the tip list. Story. Readers expect story. Readers expect character, plot, drama, conflict and resolution, no matter what. Early interactive fiction can be criticized for not delivering story, in favor of LOTS of choices. Good interactive fiction delivers both story and choice.

It's useful to consider interactive fiction as a set of connected short stories. Your stories share the same beginning, but you decide to what degree the choices take them further away from the starting point. *Deadline Delivery* is set in a dystopian flooded city where you play the role of a messenger. It uses closely linked stories with similar key events occurring in more than one storyline, although this *You Say Which Way* delivers different storylines, the author, Peter Friend, maintains a core timeline. To reinforce this, he interweaves some events which, depending on which path you take, give you different roles in the events of the day. Again, depending on which path you take, the events turn out differently. By contrast, my book *In the Magician's House,* takes the reader on vastly different adventures, depending on which direction they choose to take. There are almost no parallel timelines. As a writer this gives you a lot more freedom.

The classic storytelling arc resolves a problem introduced early in the narrative. In *Dragons Realm,* where the reader is chased into a fantasy world, most of the stories play out different resolutions to the real problem of bullying. The problem is introduced in the very first section. *Lost in Lion Country* goes one better and introduces its problem in the title! Each story ends in getting you safely home (or not!).

Although an interesting problem is full of potential for many resolutions, a single problem may reduce the likelihood that the reader will go back to explore more story. As a writer, I find I enjoy working on a project where I can embed a lot of different stories without being compelled to solve one early dilemma. Many of our books introduce conflict *after* the first choice is made. Instead, the first section has a world building function from which multiple stories can spring. For instance *Secrets of Glass Mountain* introduces a different planet in the opening chapter and the first decision is a career choice.

Moving through non-linear story requires a different cognitive task for a reader. If the story doesn't flow logically, then readers get confused and give up. Make sure your reader never doubts they have arrived at the right destination after making a choice.

The elements of style and architecture outlined in this manual are designed to give the reader a seamless story experience where they can enjoy their involvement and want to come back for more.

SETTING

Exploring a new world in interactive fiction is as interesting to a reader as the stories. *In the Magician's House* started out as a place in a different story, but as I wrote about it, I wanted to stay in the house and explore. I believe it is popular because of the promise in the title: come and find out what is in a magician's house.

Second person narrative can feel cold if your world isn't fully developed. For good ideas on writing place, try looking through travel books. They specialize in providing enticing images for a reader, and give readers a feeling of 'being there'. They tend to be written in second person too! You need enough information to prompt 'dream equivalent detail' for the reader. By this, I mean enough of a skeleton that the reader begins to form their own pictures of the world you have introduced.

The description of your story world can be dropped in as your character enters new spaces, turns corners or opens doors. It can also be part of the description around new characters they meet. If the surroundings are somewhat familiar, add enough detail to reinforce a world they might know. For instance, when you become *Lost in Lion Country* the author reinforces that it's hot and dusty (because water is going to be an issue), that trees are sparse and other places to take shelter are far away.

In *Between the Stars,* the steampunk spaceship is not a place the reader will be familiar with so I needed to add a lot of detail. I did this by starting the character in a small space (your sleep pod) and then added more detail as new spaces were revealed. This is equivalent to panning out with a movie camera.

When there wasn't a lot of story, I was happy to explore a space or place as long as it delivered new experience and I got good images and delight from that experience. At the end of a story you can hint that returning to try new choices will reveal more of the world.

ALL ABOUT CHOICE

Choice is the fundamental difference between interactive fiction and regular fiction. You'll need to master choice if you want to engage and enthrall your readers. Choice is part of a reader contract you enter into with interactive fiction. You must present choice on a regular basis throughout the story, and it has to be real choice.

Before I wrote any interactive fiction, I read a lot of it. I mapped and color-coded each book. I looked at how long each section of text was. I thought about the different sorts of choices I was given. I came up with an indicator for how satisfied I was with each individual story track.

I quickly discovered that choice could delight or frustrate me.

Satisfying choices niggle pleasantly in the reader's mind. They are what make you return, wondering what would have happened if you'd made that other choice.

At the beginning of a *You Say Which Way* book there is usually a memorable and equally weighted choice. A great example of this is found in *Secrets of Glass Mountain*. In that story, you first choose between two careers. You could be a Slider or a Miner. As a Slider, you will travel the planet on special skis, risking injury on treacherous slopes of black glass. If you choose mining, you could discover blue diamonds and become rich beyond belief. These equally weighted but very different propositions give the reader a real feeling of choice and involvement. I've often heard kids tell me after reading this book, "I was a Slider *and* a Miner." This demonstrates that they were curious and went back to try another choice that delivered value.

After the equally weighted choice, present a choice that relates to the storyline you are developing, building a sense that your decisions will shape the unfolding drama. Later, as the story develops, you can have choices with 'consequence' or even death. Initially it's important to develop the setting and possible stories. Whereas the first choice can be very divergent (Slider vs Miner) and allow you to split to two very different stories, the second section is more likely to outline a problem in the world you've entered and the second choice can offer alternative paths towards the resolution of that problem. These solution choices don't directly take you to an ending, they set up the scene for conflict and resolution. Solution choices create a deeper sense of involvement for the reader.

Choices in interactive fiction should be a bit like life. What if you had headed off overseas at 19? What if you'd studied something different? What if you'd never had kids? What if you'd kept that old clunker you first drove – what would it be worth today?

The least satisfying choices in interactive fiction are what I call 'left or right' choices. These choices don't provide a dilemma for the reader, they don't empower the reader to take part in the story and they aren't particularly memorable. Readers returning to 'left or right' choices may not recall their previous choice. If the reader finds themselves back on the same story branch they are likely to give up.

Sometimes it can be hard to interrupt great story to split it with a choice. If you feel you need to add a choice, but you don't want to deliver a split in your story, you could segue, offer a death, or offer a circular path.

A segue choice offers the reader the chance to travel across the story to an entirely different storyline. For example, after you become a dolphin in *Between the Stars* you get the option to stay as your human self on the spaceship or explore a water planet as a dolphin. Most readers will choose the more adventurous option. The choices aren't equal and I don't expect the reader to worry about what might have happened if they hadn't taken the dolphin path. So, later, after a good few dolphin adventures and some clues about what might be happening back on the spaceship, I offer the segue choice to find out what is happening back at the spaceship. By making this offer a few times, it sits in the reader's memory that there's a branch they haven't explored. Importantly, I also get to break up some long story sequence with an option I'm not expecting readers to take up straight away.

In the case of the 'meanwhile-back-on-the-spaceship' storyline, I was keen to seed the idea it was there because I'd written a spoof Sherlock Holmes thread (I was binge-watching *Elementary* at the time) and what could be better than Sherlock Holmes in space?

Offering a <u>death</u> does the same task (of providing a promised choice) but without the complication of linking to another story. You give the reader the option of choice but with an obviously unequal life vs death outcome. Your reader is satisfied they have had a choice and, if they avoid death, they've made 'the right one'. Unless of course they want to die, in the safe environment of reading a story.

By reading to groups, I learned that kids don't like to pick choices that break significant rules – at least when in the company of their peers. When the reader is marooned in *Once Upon an Island* and wants to be rescued, I first gave my listeners an option to burn down a shed to attract attention. They wouldn't do it because they perceived it as a morally incorrect choice. It's nice to see that fire safety messages are getting through, but I was frustrated because a great story lay down that path. In the end, I changed the choice to setting fire to a woodpile – straight away kids started voting for that option.

A <u>circular path</u> provides two ways to progress to the *same place* in the story. When you use circular paths you need to consider the reader's response to them. It might be frustrating for the diligent reader to go back to an enticing choice only to find it leads them back to the same story. To avoid disappointment I like to tell the reader that their choice would get them to this place either way, e.g. here from *Between the Stars:*

> Revived from the meal, you quickly figure out the co-ordinates to land the explorer. If you hadn't stopped to eat, it would have taken longer.

In the example, the reader should understand they don't need to go back and explore another path because they will come to the same place. Don't offer this type of choice too often in a book, or too early, otherwise readers may think their choices don't count. These 'parallel stories' are best used in the final sections of a story when you don't want to create another major branch.

At the end of a story, offer a circular choice to go back to a major pivot point in the story as well as the option to check the List of Choices. For example, in *Mystic Portal*, the reader can choose to ride a seahorse in a race or ride a turtle on an underwater tour. At the end of all the turtle stories, you have the choice to go back and ride a seahorse, and vice versa. It is understood that you can enjoy a different story and come back to this place in the book.

Circular choices are useful to limit the spread of your tracks. You can imagine the structure of your book as a braided river running to the sea; the more splits you have, the larger and more complicated the story becomes. But by offering a choice back to another part of the story, one of your streams runs back into another and narrows the spread of stories.

A circular choice can be used to send a reader back through a section.

For instance:
- To give them a chance to get to a great story thread that you expect they might miss
- They may have failed a task or puzzle and so they are sent back to a certain point as punishment
- They are lost and need to return to a previous section.
- They need to learn a lesson or develop skills. Making a particular choice may take them back to the same scene again and again until they make a wiser decision or develop those skills needed later in the story. In the story I'm currently writing, the cat must learn to read before it can leave the magician's house.

A circular choice might send the reader in circles but it does not necessarily mean you circle back to the *same source text*. I tied myself in knots in my first book rewriting sections so that they could be read from multiple threads. When I tried to make a section work for two tracks I invariably streamlined the information and supplied a less satisfying reader experience. Worse, circling back so that a chapter can do double duty can lead to errors. In one of the first interactive fiction books I edited, I found that a double-duty scene assumed the reader had picked up a handy tool in both paths but they actually only found the tool on one pathway into that scene. At this point, I discovered the value in subtle variation. It is better to copy and paste a section and customize it for each path, rather than angst over what the reader already knows from multiple paths.

If there is a good chance the reader has experienced the text before (for instance when the reader gets lost or 'sent back to the beginning'), I truncate the new text to avoid reading fatigue.

TIP: In interactive fiction, you can write two sections that are similar but different. The section the reader arrives at depends on their previous choices. The reader may not be aware that they are getting a shorter version of a chapter. I think of these as <u>recap sections</u>.

Lastly, a word about too much choice: Too much choice reduces your ability to develop stories. This is something Edward Packard worried about when writing *Choose Your Own Adventure*. Many choices spread the story wide, but don't give you time for depth. As a reader, I avoid stories that boast a lot of endings; my suspicion (usually well-founded) is that there won't be much story to enjoy.

Disappearing choices

In much of your story, you'll probably only have two choices. But towards the end of the book a reader will often have more than two. It's important to let the reader know this (in case one or more of the choices are on a following page). Here is an example from *Dinosaur Canyon*:

> Which of these three choices do you want to make?
> Do you:
> Go into the abandoned mine shaft after the poachers?
> Go up the hill away from the poachers?
> Or
> Go to the list of choices and read another section?

An alternative to foreshadowing the number of choices is to add a page break before each choice. That will ensure the choices start on the top of a page and none are lost. I don't use extra page breaks because I think they disconnect the choices from the experience of the story – but the choice is yours.

WRITING CHOICES

Not all interactive fiction provides a list of choices to the reader. For a lot of adult interactive fiction the fun of the 'game' is to navigate through the text and hyperlinks. Personally, if there isn't much logic to this, I don't get a lot of reader satisfaction. I'm a fan of the sort of interactive fiction where my choices affect the consequences.

Talk to people who read *Choose Your Own Adventure* and *Pick a Path* paper books when they were young and you'll often hear something like this:

"I used to have a finger in the last choice so I could go back, then a finger at the next choice and then I'd have fingers all through the book!"

And

"I used to love cheating and leaving my fingers in the book."

Or

"I'd write down the page numbers in the back for the big choices."

Kids like a navigation tool, a way to get back and try again without starting from the beginning. By having a table of contents (list of choices), readers can easily pick where they want to go. They can also see what sections they've missed.

Here's something else I hear a lot from adults remembering back, and kids who are reading *You Say Which Way* today:

"I like to read every path."

I do too.

I buy a lot of interactive fiction on Amazon. Even when it is really well-written, I don't want to re-read to try to find tracks I haven't taken. I want to start re-reading a little way into the story. A List of Choices or table of contents (or whatever you want to call it) gives the reader the ability to put virtual fingers between the pages.

You can make the List of Choices easy or obscure to navigate.

Our readers are mainly aged 8 – 12 so we often title our headers like this:

You've climbed the cliff

Keep the secret to yourself

You've joined the baboon troupe

You let the spiders into the spaceship

Switch on the light

This might seem obvious, but when I edit people's first interactive fiction I generally see writers using linear fiction's conventions for chapter headings. With linear fiction we tend to title about what is going to happen, often obscurely.

When creating interactive fiction, which will have a List of Choices, you should check through the headings to ensure they are meaningful and help remind the reader of important pivot points. Each heading needs to be an additional hook into reading more. When I find headings that don't remind me about the choices in the story, I change them.

As I'm writing interactive fiction in Microsoft Word, I have the navigation pane open so I can see all the headings. This is also known as the document map in earlier versions of Microsoft Word, and lists all the headings in your document. That really helps my mind keep track of the story. Sometimes it helps me see that I've written a bunch of meaningless choices. I go back and try and make them more enticing.

You should present choice in a consistent way. I suggest using a repeating lead-in phrase so the reader recognizes it is time to choose.

Example:

It's time for you to make a decision. Do you:
Keep following the creek in the hope of finding the Maasai village?
Or:
Stick with the baboon troupe for protection?

Time to die!

Blair Polly and I have a saying about 'dead ends' in the *You Say Which Way* books: Death is okay if it's done the right way.

The right way:
- Death comes after an obviously unwise choice
- Or a cowardly choice
- Or repeatedly risky decision making – particularly if you are risking the lives of others
- Or the boring choice
- Or sometimes when you are being selfish or mean
- Or early on to show that death can and will happen
- And to be funny

Choices have consequences. Poor choices can have dire consequences. When I began to analyze interactive fiction, I felt disappointed if I died unexpectedly or unjustly. Later, as I read different scenarios to my beta groups, I found out they didn't like to be surprised by death either. Readers approach *You Say Which Way* stories like puzzles.

The reader contract goes something like this:
- If I make dumb choices then you can kill me off.
- If I make smart choices, I stay alive.
- If I get killed off unexpectedly, I get a link to another option immediately, and don't have to find my way back.

But know this: kids enjoy dying. Readers often take silly risks just because they can, even knowing it's not the brightest thing to do. They like dying safely from the comfort of their couch or bed or on the ride to school. When you ask your beta readers about your book, ask them if they tried dying at all – I bet you they did.

Dying, it turns out, is a guilty pleasure of the interactive fiction reader. Readers especially enjoy dying if they learn that they can easily pick up where they left off. Here are some examples of death endings in various *You Say Which Way* stories:

Death scene from *Once Upon an Island:*

This death scene happens at a decisive point in the story when going for a swim is a ridiculous thing to do. (A humorous death by giant squid is a common occurrence in this book.)

You have decided to take a swim.

(Background: You've decided to take a swim even though there is an imminent reason why you shouldn't. This was a dumb decision.)

It's a hot day and the lapping of salt water on your feet feels delicious. The sand beneath the water has been warmed by the sun and squishes like chocolate pudding between your toes as you wade in. While Max and Stella are kitting up with snorkels and masks, you dive under a wave and swim out into the bay. Max and Stella dive under and when they come back up they tell you about fish they see. They muck about, flicking seaweed at each other. The three of you move out deeper and deeper.

"It's about two miles to the bottom out here," says Stella.

They dive back down again, and you feel one of them tickling your leg – their fingers feel like a snake. When Stella and Max surface a few feet away, they're yelling and waving. Hang on – what's that grabbing your leg?

A huge tentacle writhes up out of the water and turns towards you. It clamps onto your arm.

"It's a giant squid!" Stella yells in panic.

The last thing you think, as you are dragged into the depths, is how incredibly rare a death like this must be.

Glub, glub, glub.

Well, that's the end of this part of your story. What a way to go!

Stopping for a swim was a bad idea. Do you want a do over?
It's time for you to make another decision. Do you:
Want to go back to your last decision?
Or
Choose another chapter to read from the list of choices?

Here's a different way to handle death, from *Creepy House*. In the backstory, you just moved into a new house and your cat has run away. You're in bed, and you left the bedroom window open, hoping your cat would return. SOMETHING CREEPY has come into your room. You've got the choice to stay in bed with the light off, or get up and switch on the light to see what it is.

I felt it was early enough in the book to humorously kill the reader off. It also appears in the 'Read Inside' kindle preview, so I was hoping that over-protective parents would gain trust in how scary the book *isn't* from this treatment.

Handy hint: Use indents and a change of font to make text appear like a newspaper column.

You have decided to get out of bed.

Local Family Eaten By Wild Animal

A local family was eaten alive in their home on Saturday night. Police said the murderous rampage started when one of them stupidly turned on their bedroom light to find out what was making the noise under their bed.

"Everyone knows you don't do that," investigating Detective, Kahn Ivor, said. "You stay in bed and hope the monster moves on."

Wild life expert Terri Trimmings was stalking the tiger after it escaped from a local secret laboratory. "Some kid left their window open and the tiger has just slunk in there to hide. It would have been frightened and tired and disorientated. Oh, and drug crazed too. It would have wanted a safe place to sleep off the injection we gave it and then head for the hills. Instead we got carnage and now people will want to put the animal down. The tiger is the real victim in all of this."

Local realtor Mr. Ford Closeur said he didn't think the accident would affect property prices on the street. "If anything, it's put our neighborhood on the map." He is handling the sale of the house and says the blood stains will easily come out of the carpet. Mr. Closeur is new to the area himself after the mysterious disappearance of four realtors in the past two years. "They probably found themselves a bargain or two and retired. Being a realtor is an exciting job."

A memorial service for the family is likely to be canceled as they were new to the neighborhood and nobody knew them that well. "They didn't even come over and introduce themselves before they got killed," said local resident, Ima Prodnoser. "Not great manners."

That's the end of this part of the story. Don't you wish you'd stayed in bed? Try this link to find out what happens if you do.

Stay in bed?

Or

Go back to the beginning and try another path?

And then there are deaths that are the result of extremely bad judgment. Here is an excerpt from *Lost in Lion Country*.

You have decided to fill your water bottle from the stagnant pool.

The water looks a bit dirty, but you're thirsty and it's the only water you've found since you were left behind. Using your hand, you sweep the insects off the surface and lower your bottle into the water. The water has bits of plant material and other things floating around in it, but at least it's wet.

You have a couple sips to try it out. It doesn't taste quite as bad as it looks. After drinking your fill, you top up the bottle and put it in your daypack before slinging your spear back over your shoulder and moving off.

After climbing the creek bank, you have a look around to get your bearings. Leaving the creek bed and heading north seems the best plan. Maybe you'll reach the village before it gets dark. The winding creek is making your journey much longer than it would be if you were walking in a direct line.

You walk across the savannah quickly, scanning the terrain as you go. Off in the distance you see a large group of antelope grazing. Thankfully, no predators are in sight.

Walking is easier now that you've left the uneven ground of the creek bed, but it is hot, and you're thirsty.

Sweat drips down your forehead and back. The more you drink, the thirstier you get. Your mouth stays dry no matter how much water you have. Before you know it, your bottle is almost empty.

You don't feel very well. Your stomach hurts and your vision is getting blurry. The next thing you know, you're on your knees throwing up into the dust.

The water must have been contaminated. Now you're wishing you'd never had a drink.

As you throw up again, you drop to one knee. You've never felt so sick in your life. By the time you finish throwing up, your forehead is burning with fever. You curl up in a ball on the ground to try to make the pain in your stomach go away.

You're getting dizzy and feel like you're about to faint. Then blackness closes in.

Unfortunately, this part of your story is over. You made a bad decision by drinking contaminated water. Hopefully someone will find you before a predator does.

It is time for you to make a decision. Would you like to:

Go back to the very beginning of the story and take another path?

Or:

Go back to your last decision and make a different choice?

WRITING IN SECOND PERSON

Writing in second person allows the reader to become the central character of the story. Your job, and an essential part of the reader contract, is to maintain the illusion throughout the story.

Avoid giving your main character particular attributes such as:

- Gender
- Family make up
- Age
- Ethnicity
- Location
- Physical attributes

Instead, build up a sense of the person through thoughts and reactions to the situation they find themselves in.

Gender is often the most difficult attribute for the second person writer to neutralize. At first, it can seem hard to do, but after a while it becomes second nature. You'll have your evil nemesis yelling out to "grab the kid in the red hat" rather than "stop that girl" in no time. As a writer trying not to perpetuate gender stereotypes I have found writing gender neutral stories to have stretched and challenged me.

A gender neutral nickname can be a nice workaround trick if there is a need for you to be named. Eileen Mueller names her character 'The Great Zeebongi' through a branch of her book *Dragons Realm* which adds a lot of humor and allows the character to be introduced to a series of other characters.

When I was studying books that were published in the 70s and 80s I often found gender references that didn't need to be there – a particular bugbear are front covers with middle class European boys on them. Apparently, nobody told the cover designer that the main character wasn't always going to be a younger version of himself. (Not that I'm assuming the illustrators were men.)

Lack of family fit can break immersion as much as breaking out of gender neutral language. Try using 'your family' instead of 'your parents' (which implies two parents when lots of kids these days only live with one). It's best not to use references to Mom or Dad either – you don't know if your reader has a mom or dad. Instead of inventing a little brother or sister use a sidekick like the neighbor who has tagged along, your friend, or a kid who lives in the area the story is set.

It's helpful to think of the second person character on a continuum of proximity to the reader. At one end the character is the reader directly, at the other end the reader is invited to play the role of a character.

READER = YOU <<--------------->> READER PLAYS A ROLE

In *Deadline Delivery,* author Peter Friend gives the reader the role of a messenger in a flooded anarchical city. It is very clear that the role the reader is playing is not an extension of the reader's own life. Because the reader is playing a role, there is scope for their character to know things and do things that the reader could not know, without a loss of credibility. Because the reader is playing a role, Peter Friend gives their character thoughts and, because of this, more character.

In *Between the Stars* the reader plays the role of a petty thief sentenced to transportation on a spaceship in a steam punk world. The reader gradually learns more of their character's background, but there is also a certain amount of mystery to the character as people who sleep gradually lose their memories and, as we discover, can become vessels for the minds of others.

Complete fantasy worlds and role-play characters offer the writer more scope to embellish the second person character. It is still important to neutralize age and sex and ethnicity and anything else that is jarringly different from the reader.

Many of the *You Say Which Way* books start from the other end of the second person spectrum (READER = YOU). In *Danger on Dolphin Island* the reader has arrived with their family (of unspecified type!) at a tropical resort. The story takes place in the present time in a real location. *Once Upon an Island* has a similar beginning – you choose to travel to New Zealand. While the opportunity to travel to different countries might not be open of many of our readers, they are plausible ideas. The reader enters the story with a greater sense of their own participation as opposed to a role they are playing.

When writing your own interactive fiction, think about the reader's distance from the story setup – are you lifting off from their life (READER = YOU) or offering them a role to play (READER PLAYS A ROLE)? The answer will dictate how much detail the second person character can begin with.

THE SIDEKICK

Like a TV show, an interactive story is helped by a sidekick or two. They can ask dumb questions and have things explained to them. They can argue with you about your decisions, they can back you up, they can give you courage, they can provide information and they can actually get you into trouble. A side kick allows you to break up description with dialogue.

A sidekick can stay in the adventure all the way through, or you can introduce different sidekicks for different branches. In *Creepy House* the closest the reader gets to a sidekick is their pet cat, because being alone adds to the creep factor.

We also chose not to have a fulltime sidekick for *Lost in Lion Country* because there was a lot of action and we thought a friend would slow things down.

However the reader does meet a number of people for short parts of their African adventure. This allows these other characters to impart information, offer guidance, save you from an attacking lion and help you thwart rhino poachers.

A faithful sidekick can even be a duo – several of our books have a brother and sister duo who can operate independently or as your team. A sidekick can even make decisions now and again as, just in real life, we sometimes defer to others.

Your sidekick can undergo a transformation during story tracks, reflecting the obstacles the story has thrown at you both. Sidekicks provide a lot of personality while the character of 'you' is essentially blank. (Although your reactions to the sidekick reveal your character during the story.)

Meet Matilda, the sidekick from *The Sorcerer's Maze Time Machine*:

The door is ajar so Matilda gives it a shove and walks into the laboratory. "Hey," she says over her shoulder, "come and look at this."

"Are we allowed?" you ask, stepping cautiously through the doorway. "This area's probably off limits."

"I didn't see a sign," Matilda says, rubbing a finger along the edge of a stainless steel bench as she proceeds further into the brightly lit room. "And if they're going to leave the door open…"

The lab's benches are crammed with electrical equipment.

You move further into the room. "What do you think all this stuff does?"

Matilda wanders down the narrow space between two benches, looking intently at the equipment as she goes. "I dunno. But they don't skimp on gear, do they?"

She prods a brick-sized black box with a row of green numbers glowing across it. "I wonder what this does." She picks it up.

Tiny lights glow above a circular dial. On the top of the box is an exposed circuit board made of copper and green plastic.

"Looks like an old digital clock." You say, pointing at the first number in the row. "See, here's the hours and minutes, then the day, the month and the year." You pull out your cell phone and check the time. "Yep. It's spot on."

"That makes sense," Matilda says. "But what's the dial for?"

"Beats me. To set an alarm, maybe?"

Matilda rubs her finger along a curved piece of copper tubing fitted neatly into one end of the box. "So what's this coil for? Doesn't look like any timer I've ever seen."

She turns the box over to find a sticky label underneath. It reads:

HANDS OFF - PROPERTY OF THE SORCERER

She turns the box back over and starts fiddling with the dial.

You take a step back. "I don't think that's a good–"

Well, you can tell that Matilda is going to get you into all sorts of trouble. The main quality a sidekick needs is to be someone you can talk to, so you can voice your thoughts. Sidekicks don't have to be human, but if they are, they should be about the intended reader's age to maintain the autonomy of your own character. Childhood is a very hierarchical experience. Introducing older characters and adults works against one of the biggest reader contracts in children's literature: the main character will be autonomous.

In all classic children's fiction, one of the first jobs of the writer is to 'orphan' the protagonist – that's you. Severed from parental control, the young reader can experience autonomy – a key pleasure for those whose everyday life is usually highly supervised. If the protagonist is not orphaned they are placed under the benignly neglectful control of absentminded professors or adults unskilled in the monitoring role of careful parents.

Here's another type of sidekick – this one is an 'uneven sidekick'. They look up to you, and you are definitely in charge. They'll have skills that come in handy but are no threat to the reader's leadership. They give the reader a chance to try the role of an elder sibling.

Meet Paulie from Blair Polly's *Dinosaur Canyon*:

"My tent's up, Mister Jackson, so I'm off to look around."

The teacher nods. "Make sure you fill in the logbook with your intentions. Oh, and who're you teaming up with? Remember our talk on safety – you're not allowed to go wandering about alone. And watch out for rattlesnakes."

You look at the chaos around camp. Rather than being interested in dinosaur fossils, which is the main reason for this trip, most of your fellow students are puzzling over how their borrowed tents work or complaining about the cell phone reception. Camping equipment is strewn everywhere. Apart from you, Paulie is the only one who's managed to get his tent up so far.

"Hey, Paulie. I'm heading out. Want to tag along?"

Paulie points to his chest. "Who? Me?"

Paulie's not really a friend. He's a year behind you at school, but at least he seems interested in being here. He's even got a flag with a picture of a T. Rex working at the front counter of a burger joint, flying over his tent. Chuckling, you ponder the silliness of a short-armed dinosaur flipping burgers

"Yeah, you. Get a move on." You walk over and write in the camp's log book. *Going west towards hills with Paulie. Back in time for dinner.*

"What are we going to do?" Paulie asks.

"Explore those hills," you say, pointing off into the west. "Quick, grab your pack and let's go … before Mr. J or one of the parents decide to come along."

As Paulie shoves a few supplies in his bag, you look across the scrubland towards the badly-eroded hills in the distance. It's ideal country for finding fossils. Erosion is the fossil hunter's best friend. Who knows what the recent rains have uncovered for a sharp-eyed collector like you?

You'll have a sense of responsibility for Paulie during your adventures that will add gravitas to your decisions. The socially maturing reader may also consider the inconsistencies of an age-based hierarchy as Paulie's knowledge and advice help you make decisions.

Lastly, here's one of my favorite sidekicks. In this branch you're a dolphin and you've been sent off to explore a mostly aquatic planet for possible settlement. I thought it might help if you had a dolphin friend.

Here's where you meet your dolphin sidekick from *Between the Stars* for the first time:

"The ship is close to a new planet," Dr. Alan says. "It's mostly covered in water. We've decided a dolphin is the best scout for this largely aquatic environment. There are other planets in this solar system, but for the mission to be successful, we need to pick the best one to settle on. You're going to be the first explorers."

"Lucky us," whistles your tank companion in the language of dolphins.

Her clicking is pleasing to your ears. You've never noticed before how gruff and unmelodic humans sound when they talk.

"Hello," you whistle back.

"Hello, Proudfin," says the dolphin next to you.

"Proudfin?"

"That's what I'm calling you. Any objection?"

"That's fine … Longtail," you say.

From the quick series of clicks she makes, you know she likes the name you just gave her. It has two meanings. Not only does the other dolphin have a long tail, but the tales of your adventures will be carried a long way.

"Listen up, you two," Dr. Alan continues. "A small spaceship, an 'explorer', is to be sent to the planet below. The explorer will also carry robots. They will build a radio station for you to broadcast back to the *Victoria*. You will be placed in special tubes of sleep jelly. The jelly will help cushion you in space and also provide oxygen in the same way it does when you sleep. Once you land on the new planet, you'll explore and report back via the radio station."

Currently I'm writing from the point of view of a cat and experiencing the limitations of a creature that doesn't really speak. I've added sidekicks that speak to you and a few you can speak with (for instance, I've decided wolves and dragons can speak with cats).

CHARACTERS

While the second person character, 'you', might not have much detail, that doesn't mean you won't be surrounded by well-imagined and interesting characters. As a writer of second person prose, I've often found that the actors in my stories seem more vivid to me than when I write in third person.

Characters play an important role in interactive fiction by developing the thoughts and experiences of the reader. They draw out the second person character. Dialogue is one of the methods that storytellers use to 'show' rather than 'tell'.

Inexperienced writers often introduce 'casts of thousands' to their work. Readers struggle to meet a crowd of people on the page and form mental pictures of them. It is confusing and disappointing to invest time imagining someone who has no role to play. In interactive fiction, over-populating your stories is even more confusing. The reader is constantly vigilant for meaning to help them make the next choice.

- Only introduce characters who have a part to play. If a character doesn't have a large part to play, minimize their description and definitely don't name them.
- In general, introduce characters as they are needed. You can drip-feed people into threads where they have a role to play, and minimize them in others.
- However, it can be very pleasant for a reader to catch the shadow of a character in one thread, where they aren't important, and find them more fully realized in another where they are part of the story.
- In interactive fiction, dialogue is a great way to get to know a character, just like in real life.

EASTER EGGS

An Easter egg is a term for hidden material for the reader. The name originated from Easter egg hunts. Film buffs use the term to describe 'insider' material planted in movies and bonus material found in DVDs and trailers. Interactive fiction has great potential for Easter eggs.

It could be extra story, jokes, promotional material such as bonus previews, or more detailed information about the setting or other characters the reader has met in their journey. In the *You Say Which Way* series, a link to the Easter egg is often tucked into the List of Choices so the sharp-eyed reader can find it.

DITCHING SECOND PERSON

Second person is conventional, but it isn't compulsory. You *can* tell interactive stories using third person. If you use third person, you'll discover you can use multiple characters.

If you tell a third person story, you still want to bring the reader with you. You'll need a strong, consistent method to arrive at choices and offer them to the reader. One method I'm using in a story I have underway is to give the reader a choice as to which character they follow. I'm offering choices at points of departure, e.g.

> There was the sound of a turning page, and Hannah was gone. Straightaway, the queen missed the baby terribly and wanted to call them back. She remembered the necklace that Hannah had given her. Could it really help? She put the chain around her neck, and as the pendent hit her throat, she forgot she'd ever had a baby at all … and so did everyone else in the kingdom.
>
> The queen put the book back on the high shelf. Clambering down, she had a niggling feeling she'd forgotten about something. She reached for her necklace and she felt better. A hunting horn sounded below, so she set off to greet the king.
>
> Gentle reader, it is time to make a choice – do you want to follow the queen down the stairs, or would you prefer to find out what happened to the baby?
>
> Follow the baby
>
> Or
>
> Follow the queen

The choices in the extract above occur at a pivot point in the story where two main characters go their separate way. Both will be instrumental in solving the book's problem, and at various stages I'll provide a gateway to travel back and forth to each character's story. I'm planning to offer some segue choices and also offer the same story (when both characters are together) from different points of view. I'm envisaging the story to be a little like interactive theatre.

Note: It would still be possible to write this as a second person story. You could offer the reader the choice to take on the character's role, or give them a role that will remain close to the characters, for instance, a servant to the queen.

ADDING NON-FICTION CONTENT

In interactive fiction, you can approach non-fiction content in different ways:

- Woven directly into the story
- Optional links to a glossary to give more information
- Puzzle inside story

It's extremely important that you fact check. Keep a list of facts and their sources for your editor or proofer.

'Info-dumps' are boring, but if facts are woven into the story for a reason, kids enjoy it. Conversations with sidekicks provide a good way to weave information into the story. But don't be preachy. Commonly we'll use a hyperlink in the main body of a story section to invite a reader to find out more about something.

For instance, in *Dinosaur Canyon* there are references to different dinosaurs. Links takes you to facts about each dinosaur and then a return link is provided to get you back to the scene you've just left. This exploits one of the advantages of eReading.

In *Once Upon an Island* I added a choice at the very beginning that allows you to completely opt out of going to New Zealand. Your reluctance for adventure sees you learning math all summer. I used the first choice as a sort of training ground for readers new to interactive fiction. I worried that I'd made math sound bad, so I added some fun questions that are teasers for the rest of the story and for another one of our books, *Lost in Lion Country*.

Question One:
Giant squid from the waters around New Zealand can drag someone of your weight and strength down to the bottom of a three mile trench in ten minutes. How many minutes would it take for two giant squid to drag you down to a watery grave?

Question Two:
You find a device which moves you backwards and forwards in time. You discover that you move back one hundred years every time you hit the back button and you move forward fifty years every time you hit the forward button. You travel back 300 years and find yourself being chased by a giant eagle. The Haast's eagle was the largest eagle that ever lived, and has been extinct for two hundred years. How many times do you have to hit the forward button to avoid being a meal for a giant eagle?

Question Three:
While *Lost in Lion Country* you find yourself left alone with the safari picnic basket. There are 50 ham sandwiches inside the basket. One hyena will be satisfied after 10 ham sandwiches and will head off to sleep in the sun. How many hyenas can you hold off until help arrives?

(If you want the answers, you can check out the story!)

Feedback from these questions confirmed that trivia and puzzles were welcomed in interactive fiction for kids. Some kids even send us proposed questions. Where possible, we weave them into our stories.

Embedding optional hyperlinked facts, rather than putting too many facts into a story, means the reader can decide if they want to break out of the story or not. The fact-finding reader can go straight to the facts. The reader immersed in the story can find the facts later when they play around with the List of Choices.

Blair Polly has created the *Sorcerer's Maze* stories. These are very fact-driven. In each 'adventure quiz', the reader has to answer questions and solve puzzles correctly to move forward through the story. The reader doesn't die, but there can be a degree of frustration if you don't get the answers right and end up in some endless loop with parrots laughing at you, or in a multidimensional hallway where you have to go through a series of doors in a particular sequence to escape.

Sorcerer's Maze still contains a story, and you have to attain a goal via your actions, so these books are still technically interactive fiction, but rather than having multiple endings, every track funnels into a common point, and readers terminate at a common, successful ending (eventually).

When I think about books I've enjoyed as an adult, I realize that I like books where I learn something while enjoying a good story. For instance, in the book *Larry's Party* by Canadian author Carol Shields, Larry creates labyrinth hedges for a living. It was a window into a niche horticultural world. Another adult book I loved was *The Piano Shop on the Left Bank* by Thad Carhart – it took me to the city and culture of Paris, the history of pianos and an insight into playing music. Currently I'm reading *Stim* by New Zealand author Kevin Berry, which allows me to understand people on the autistic spectrum. My point is, good books are full of information. The potential to learn facts from a fictional story continues into adult reading.

LINKING TO CONTENT ON THE WEB

This is an area of interactivity you should be wary of.

We don't usually add external links to *You Say Which Way* books. Most parents and teachers would expect a book to be self-contained. Families and schools have a variety of internet policies, all motivated to keep kids safe online. The best way to adhere to those policies is to stay away from external links.

The exceptions we make are a few clear signposts to our other books on Amazon. We mostly do this by providing a montage of book covers rather than links. After consultation with parents, we have also provided clear links to where *You Say Which Way* books can be bought or borrowed on Amazon, but we don't link to webpages outside of Amazon.

Many authors of adult books offer free content to gain an email list to inform readers about their next book. These lists are usually managed by web services where mail lists are held with an external source. A children's author needs to think carefully before starting a mail list that children may subscribe to. I have made the decision not to develop a children's mailing list. What if your mailing list was on-sold or hacked and children were contacted by someone pretending to be you?

We have one specific point where readers can contact us. This is at YouSayWhichWay.com and it is used to suggest questions for further *Sorcerer's Maze* books. We manage the system without using an external mail service, have clear privacy statements, ask kids to check with their parents before sending us a message and, importantly, do not retain their information indefinitely.

If you choose to interact with kids online, you should be aware of COPPA, the Children's Online Privacy Protection Act, which is a United States federal law. It is designed to protect children under the age of 13. The guidance the law gives is useful ethically as well as legally. Many web services are based in America and come under the

US legal jurisdiction. Check the fine print when you use these services to ensure that you aren't in violation of their terms and conditions regarding interactions with children. You wouldn't want to lose a we

INSPIRATION

People often ask me how I get the inspiration to write so many stories in one book. Here are some of the things that work for me:

What do kids/people like doing? While writing *In the Magician's House* I am totally guilty of first using something my mother gave me. She once told me: when you were little, when we went to visit someone, you'd ask to go to the bathroom so you could sneak around looking at the rest of their house. When I thought of a magician's house, I knew that the child in me (the adult too, to be honest) would want to explore it. I'd be asking to go to the bathroom! I started that story wanting to give the reader the ultimate experience of discovery.

I also use an awareness of this desire to see behind closed doors in *Creepy House*. It's the opposite of *In the Magician's House* because it's deliberately scary, rather than a magical adventure. But it appeals to the question: what happens behind those closed doors?

Eating is another thing kids enjoy. You'll find plenty of meal breaks in my writing and they often act as resting points between action, a time to sum up what we know so far, and add a bit more info before a choice.

What are people afraid of? *Creepy House* was my first attempt at writing horror. I hadn't really thought of writing horror before because I'm a complete scaredy-cat. I spent large chunks of my childhood watching TV from behind the couch. This turned out to be an advantage for writing scary stories. When I stared *Creepy House*, I wrote a list of the things that scared me as a kid:

- Monsters under the bed (obviously)
- Wild animals turning up
- My parents disappearing (conversely, also something I looked forward to)
- Being replaced by an evil twin

- Getting trapped somewhere
- Being eaten by sharks or alligators
- Being crushed by a giant washing machine on spin cycle

That was more than enough to start with.

Start with a dilemma or opportunity: The best example I have of a dilemma is *Lost in Lion Country.* Blair Polly and I were gleeful when we came up with that title because the whole problem of the book was there out front, right from the beginning. After that it was about brainstorming all the different ways that problem could play out.

Recycling characters: In *Between the Stars,* I enjoyed referencing HG Wells as the ship's captain, only there is something a little bit different about my Captain Wells, as readers find out early on. I don't expect kids to know the people I use, but I know I have a lot of adult readers too, so I'm giving them the pleasure of recognizing people. I call it 'the Shrek effect'. As a writer it also means I don't have to make up a character from thin air, I have a great starting point.

My daughter told me about the real historical female pirate Ching Shee. We both got very excited about her, and I gave her a feisty part in *Between the Stars.* Here's an excerpt that gives you an idea about her character:

> "You need a bird too," says Ching Shee, agreeing with your strategy. She brings her chair closer and looks at the game pieces. Her guards crowd around too. One takes off their helmet. You look at Ching Shee and you look at the guard – they could be twins. Ching Shee sees you looking.
>
> "She's one of the nearly Ching Shees – she is 'the same recipe'. She gets to be an honor guard and also to play games with me."
>
> "How do you stop from getting mixed up?" The question comes from Trig, it seems like the ice is broken and everyone has stopped being so formal.

"She does not have this," says Ching Shee, rolling up her sleeve. Her arm is tattooed with a blue dragon. The head covers her wrist and the body coils up toward her elbow. "Only one of us wears the dragon. The seventh Ching Shee only wore the dragon for three days."

"What happened to her?" you ask.

"The eighth Ching Shee happened to her," purrs Ching Shee the ninth.

From *Between the Stars* by DM Potter, Fairytale Factory, 2014.

I have no idea what the original Ching Shee was like, but reading about her certainly fired my imagination. Note: many Europeans spell the pirate Ching Shee's name as 'Ching Shih'. I decided my readers were more likely to say her name correctly if I used 'Shee', which is another variant.

Other times I enjoy creating a backstory for a historical figure. Charles Dickens makes an appearance between the pages of *In the Magician's House*. Dickens was, no doubt, motivated to write about the poor because of his own experience of hard times in Victorian England. His family spent time in a debtor's prison, and he was pulled out of school and put to work in a blacking factory. It must have been lonely and frightening. We meet Charlie and help him on his road to being an author. Young readers may never know that Charlie Dickens is based on Charles Dickens but, just like Ching Shee, he provided excellent stimulus for story.

Fairytale: I love reworking traditional fairytales and making them my own. I have reworked The Three Little Pigs, Rapunzel, Sleeping Beauty and many more. The librarian character I developed for *In the Magician's House,* and who has a bigger part to play in *The Magician's Cat*, is based on a grown-up idea of Red Riding Hood.

Ask fans: I wanted to try writing 'you' from the point of view of an animal. So, I decided I'd add a thread to the current book I was working on just to see how it went. I wasn't overly fussed which animal I'd use, so I put a question up on the Fairytale Factory's

Facebook page. The favorites were dolphin, wolf and cat. Hence the dolphin section in *Between the Stars*.

Cultural difference: My kids have Māori ancestry and are from the tribe (or, properly, 'iwi') Ngati Kahungunu. In *Between the Stars* I created an alternate history line in which the Māori of New Zealand hadn't been colonized, but had gone on to encourage indigenous people of the world to take control of their land. That meant the Victorians had looked to space to spread out and to solve their unemployment problem, rather than Australia, New Zealand, America and Canada. Well, after I'd developed this cool backstory, I figured it would be fun to explore the various approaches to space travel you might get from different cultures. *Between the Stars* mostly uses a steampunk setup which riffs off Victorian culture. When the crew of the *Victoria* meet up with explorers from Ngati Kahungunu, we find that Māori have quite a different society that has designed a different technology for space travel.

One word of caution about using different culture to inspire you – be aware of cultural appropriation. If you are dealing with a living culture, particularly a marginalized culture, have discussions with people from that culture before you start writing. They should be comfortable with what you are doing. If you can't connect with people from the culture, it would be best not to assume your story is okay.

Use a familiar setting: I once had a memorable trip to Arapawa Island. You get there by ferry across the Cook Strait, which separates the North and South islands of New Zealand. It is remote and surrounded by deep ocean. There are giant squid, whales and sharks in the waters. *Once Upon an Island* was my first *You Say Which Way* adventure. I wanted to use a place I knew to experiment with the genre. Few people in the world would have been there, so I also didn't feel constrained from imagining underground bunkers and caves and derelict farms. It was a great leaping off point.

Die: If you are ever writing along and you feel it's time to add a choice, but you don't want to split the story up, add a death option.

Don't forget your reader contract though! Make sure that the death is a logical result of a bad choice.

Brainstorm with flow charts: I map my story as I go, I'm a 'pantser' generally so my map is also a bit of a brainstorm process. I don't always use all my ideas. In fact, I often circle off a bit that I like and that becomes the story I follow. I can always leave unused ideas for another book. I enjoy creating new versions of my flowchart as I work, which probably reinforces my memory of events.

Ask your friends: While writing *In the Magician's House,* I asked people what they might find in a magician's house. Here are a few suggestions:

- From my friend Gordon, the policeman: a tube of hope
- From the chief librarian at New Zealand's parliamentary library: a portable hole
- From a cousin in Australia aged 4: a frog. What color, I asked? Red.

All of these suggestions were fantastic writing prompts. During my last class visit, the kids had all read *In the Magician's House,* so I asked them for suggestions for *The Magician's Cat.* I came away with a big to do list to work from. Incidentally, they were keen to get more backstory on the characters they had met *In the Magician's House,* and they wanted more appearances from the portable hole.

While Eileen Mueller was working on *Dragons Realm,* she brainstormed with her critique partners, school kids, and anyone who would listen!

Our author team bounce ideas off each other, as it can be difficult to come up with so many different storylines in one book. We often find that a stray comment can solve a tricky dilemma, or spark an entire branch of multiple stories.

Should interact fiction be used to teach morality?

Short answer: No.

Longer answer: If your books are preachy and moralistic, kids will see right through them. But good stories very often explore problems that interest kids. Being lost, being scared, being bullied, being poor, keeping safe, dealing with problematic friends, worrying about the environment, making choices for the future – these are all problems kids think about. These problems make great themes for books and can demonstrate that there is never just one way to approach an issue.

Dragons Realm starts off with a kid being chased by the school bullies – the Thomson twins. It's a running gag that they are actually triplets, but no one is brave enough to explain that to them. Escaping the bullies leads you to your discovery of Dragons Realm. Once in Dragons Realm plenty more story happens, depending on the choices you take, but in nearly every thread, the Thompson twins turn up and the problem bullying is explored. Bullying is a complex issue and we think *Dragons Realm* deals with a real issue in an authentic way.

The mechanics of an interactive book

LIST OF CHOICES

This is the main navigation tool for the reader. It gives the reader:

- Navigation to unexplored tracks
- The chance to choose again
- A place to go if you get lost
- Hints and motivation to read more
- And a framework for editors and proofers to check through in conjunction with a map.

If you decide to have a List of Choices, you need to make a decision about where to place it. It isn't like a traditional table of contents that you would expect to find at the front. And besides: spoilers! My recommendation is to place the List of Choices somewhere close to the front, but after the first ten percent of the book. That way it won't be part of the Amazon 'Look Inside' experience for people checking out the book.

MAPPING YOUR STORY

Map your story to provide guidance for editors and proofers. It's quite possible, depending on the complexity of your story, that a map will be a handy reference for you too.

Here is the first way I mapped my stories. Using Excel, I gave each heading a number which corresponded to the previous heading number. I used the numbers on my headings as I drafted the first edition.

I ended up with a list that looked a little like this:

0 (the starting point)
1 (the text after the first choice)
2 (the text after the second choice)
1.1 (the text from the first option after the reader picked 1)
1.2 (the text from the second option after the reader picked 1)
2.1 (I hope you get it now)
2.2
1.1.1
1.1.2 (etc.)

While this was a logical way to organize my story, my first editor and proofer didn't enjoy working with it. Some people don't find Excel very appealing. My editor requested a map to help understand the flow of the story. As luck would have it, I also had a map. I'd brainstormed using a map. I had just thought I needed to be uber systematic with my numbering system.

I also found that hyperlinks connected to sections that started with numbers broke when you removed the numbers in some versions of Word. Hours of proofing later, I vowed never to use the system again.

When I started writing with Blair Polly, we brainstormed with maps and gave each other final maps to proof and edit with. When you edit interactive fiction, you want to read thread by thread. We tend to tick off sections we've covered with a pencil on a map. Here is an example:

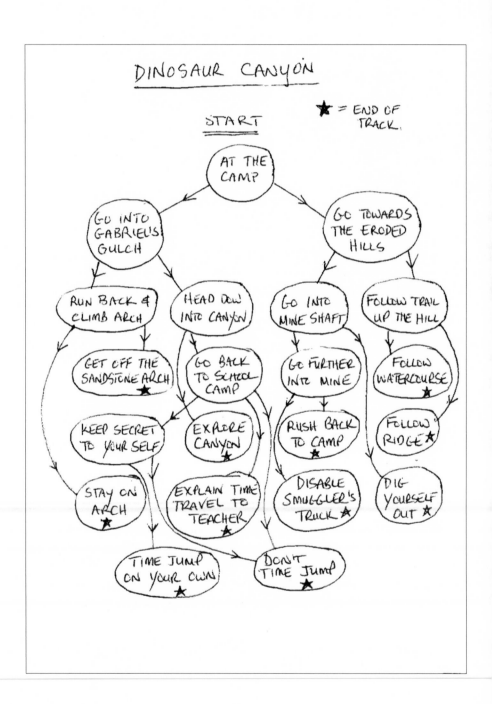

HEADINGS

Headings are important in interactive fiction.

Headings:

- reassure the reader that they have arrived at the right place
- appear in the list of choices
- back shadow the choices made, rather than foreshadow the events about to happen
- are interesting!
- and not too long! From a formatting point of view, a long heading will look poor in the list of choices as it will spread over two lines rather than one.

NAVIGATION INSTRUCTIONS

I strongly suggest you include a section that details how hyperlinks can be activated by different eReaders. Bear in mind that kids often inherit old tech – hyperlinks might be easy to touch navigate on modern tablets, but early Kindles were a lot clunkier.

Here is an example:

> All reading devices can activate the hyperlinks used in this story. Here are the most common ways:
>
> On a reading device with a cursor press UP to begin choosing, then use UP and DOWN to pick an option and the main button to select your choice. On other models press SELECT to highlight a choice and then SELECT again to activate it.
>
> On a PC use control + click.
>
> On a touch screen device, just touch your selection.
>
> If you ever see only ONE choice where you expected more, check the next page for more choices.
>
> Are you ready to go?
>
> Take me to the story.
>
> Take me to the List of Choices.

Note: In an eBook the last two lines would be hyperlinks. In paperback versions, page numbers are given after the line.

Here is an example:

> Take me to the story (**P1**)
>
> Take me to the List of Choices (**P54**)

GO BACK PAGES

Go back pages (we often insert a stop sign image) tell the reader to go back and choose. We tend to pepper these instructions into the first few sections and then trust that the reader 'gets it' and doesn't need further instruction. Here is an example:

You need to go back and make a choice.

(This example of a go-back page is a signpost for readers who have scrolled instead of choosing, telling them that they should go back to the previous page and make a decision before proceeding further.)

Editing, proofing and perfecting your book

CONSISTENCY

This doesn't just apply to interactive fiction, but your editor and proofers will thank me for it. Right from the start, it's useful to keep a record of how you are spelling or phrasing key words.

When I started this book, I decided to be consistent about how I spelt eBook, eReader, eReading etc. I decided to put all book titles in italics. I used styles in Word for the main body text and headings in Word. My editor may recommend changes to these conventions. It will be easy to make changes to styles – literally a 2-second job. It will be easy to use 'find and replace' if we decide we don't want to use a capital R in eReader. If you don't make decisions early on and note them down, you are likely to be inconsistent and have a mess to tidy up.

Handy hint: don't pick character names that are also words in another context. If you name a character 'Will' or 'Rocky' and then want to change it, you'll have to go through the book manually rather than using the 'replace all' function.

Beta testing

Most good writers have a critique group and/or a beta testing crew. I critique other people's writing and I wouldn't dream of publishing anything that hadn't had a few critical friends go through it. If you are writing for kids, however, you should also include kids in your beta reading plan.

I can't stress enough how useful and informative it is to read aloud to your audience. I started out reading to a lunchtime library audience at Thorndon School. I am so grateful to the school for letting me in! I got the kids to vote on choices and learned a LOT about choices that first day. I was also madly scribbling edits with my pencil. When I read aloud I hear my clunky writing.

I asked the kids to raise their hand if I used a word that people don't use these days. They helped me out by signaling confusing words. They also told me that Kindles have a dictionary and they used them.

I've also found it useful to watch a pair of young readers reading a draft of my work on an iPad. By pairing them up, they talk to each other and I can overhear what motivates them to make choices. I learn a lot this way.

I babysit for a few kids and offer to share my work with them. I never *make* kids listen to my work. I really want to know that the subject matter is interesting in itself. I hate to think of a kid suffering through something I've written out of politeness and I would also doubt the feedback I get.

Kids can be remarkably insightful, in spite of not having a Masters in Creative Writing. My 9-year-old neighbor Amos and I read an early draft of *Between the Stars*. You meet up with some scary shark-like creatures. I had described them as having arms.

Afterwards, Amos mused aloud: "but why do the sharks have arms, Deb?"

"You're right!" I exclaimed. "It's like a Chekhovian gun! If the sharks have arms, they really need to use them for something."

"Well," Amos said carefully, "I want to know what they use their arms for, I don't know about the gun thing."

That night I went back home and gave the sharks things to do with their arms. In one thread I had them picking at the sides of the space explorer after the two dolphins have raced inside and shut the door. The whole scene was a lot creepier knowing the sharks might find a way to get inside their shelter. In another branch, a shark baby is trapped by coral creatures. The sharks use their arms to drop rocks on the creatures from above to try to free their baby. When that doesn't work, you help with your extra armor and your laser and cut the baby free, and earn their respect. Without Amos I would never have built up those storylines. I'm also pleased I came up with an evolutionary reason the arms might be useful – thwarting the coral creatures.

If you are lucky enough to have access to schools, volunteer to read at lunchtime with the kids. I'd suggest reading other people's work as well as your own.

Learn the art of asking good questions of your beta readers. Here are some questions I typically ask:

- How did you find your way through the story? (not 'was it easy?' – just how did you do it?)
- Which section do you think was the most boring one? (permission to say a section is weak)
- What would you tell a friend that the story was about? (great for blurbs and titles and finding out what appeals most)
- What didn't I explain very well? (NOT what didn't you understand?)

When you talk to beta readers, be sure to ask them if they used the List of Choices at all. If they did, was it easy to navigate? Were there any times they went looking for something and couldn't find it?

Editing

You are unlikely to find an experienced editor of interactive fiction. You should tell your editor that you are aiming to provide good compelling story and they should treat the manuscript as a collection of short stories that could be read independently. Give your editor a hand-drawn map or your excel sheet (did I mention that I prefer maps, if you're writing for me) to help them navigate the draft and recommend they also use the navigation pane. Ask them to read through by story instead of 'from the top'. In addition to all the things an editor would usually cover, ask that they look out for:

- Any lapses in gender neutrality
- Places where the use of 'you' could be reduced
- Accidental reference to family specifics, ethnic origin, of other overly assumptive description of the reader
- Headings in the List of Choices that are not meaningful or do not highlight important pivot points.

A copy of this book would help an inexperienced editor of interactive fiction. Although we sell all over the world, eighty percent of our market is in America, so edit in American English.

PROOFING

A regular proofer goes through looking for errors and conformity with styles you have setup (such as Ebook vs eBook). All links in the book must also be tested – although this could be done by a different person. The links should be checked regularly as you write your book, but they are also the final thing that should be checked before publication. You can also ask a proofer to check your facts.

I check links by opening my file anew, so that all the hyperlinks are blue. I enable the navigation pane. Then I travel through the book checking the links. At the end of the process, I should be able to travel through and see that every hyperlink is now purple. Unchecked links would still be blue (or whatever color your package indicates unclicked links).

As I check the links, I note the section I'm in via the navigation pane. When I've traveled to the correct destination, I travel to the next link to be checked by clicking the heading *below* the choice I want to check. It's a short scroll up to the bottom of the previous page to find the next link to check.

BACKING UP AND FILE SHARING

We use Dropbox to back up our files and share files for critique, collaboration, editing and proofing. There are a number of file-sharing options out there; just remember to back up outside of your own hard drive.

Somewhere out there is a burglar who has 50k of a third-rate novel I once wrote. I guess I should be glad he or she stole it because I might still be writing YA time travel instead of interactive fiction.

Using Word to make interactive fiction

I posted on several forums when I started writing this how-to manual, asking people what questions they had. To my surprise a frequent question was what software I used and the programming skills that were needed.

Microsoft Word is incredibly useful in making interactive fiction. I'm only going to write this once: different versions of Word are different. Your mileage may vary. Just use Google if your version is not the same as the examples I give here.

If you prefer other software to Word, go right ahead – just check your editors and proofers have the same software too. I am told that Scrivener can do all of the things I list below. I have not heard the same about Google Docs, but I understand it also utilizes hyperlinks so, no doubt, it can do a variation of everything I discuss here. If you are not planning to use Word, this section should be used as a guide to get the full functionality out of your word-processing software.

Here are a few ways I use Word for *You Say Which Way* books:

STYLES

Use **styles**. You can set up the styles for your **headings** and sub-headings and body text and then if you want to change something, all you have to do is change your style. Word calls body text **normal**. Don't wait for an editor to do this for you. Set it up in the beginning. If you are submitting to someone, ask for their style guide or template and write into that.

You can also set up paragraph indents automatically. Do not use tabs or spaces. There is nothing worse than an editor having to go through and delete all your tabbed or spaced indents. Do not use old-fashioned manuscript formatting conventions, such as two spaces instead of one, or double hyphens for em-dashes.

NAVIGATION PANE

While you write, keep the **navigation pane** (or document map) open. You'll find it under the View tab for most versions of Word. The navigation pane will list all your headings and sub-headings. I like to draft complete sections in one sitting, but if I haven't finished a section when I'm saving the document, I add a few exclamation marks to the middle of headings. They stand out well in the navigation pane and remind me where I still have work to do.

Hyperlinking to headings and bookmarks

Use **hyperlinks, headings** and **bookmarks**. Word makes this very easy. You will be linking your choices to headings. Sometimes you might like to create bookmarks, which will take you to a place within a chapter. Use a bookmark when you don't want to link to a heading. Make the bookmark first so you have something to link to. Here's how:

1. To make a hyperlink, highlight a word or, more usually in interactive fiction, a choice at the end of a section.
2. From the ribbon menu, click insert hyperlink or use control+k and choose to link to 'somewhere in this document'.
3. Choose a heading (or a bookmark you have already made).
4. Bam! It's as easy as that.
5. Always test your hyperlinks as part of your proofing process, but if you ever make changes to the wording of hyperlinks you should test them immediately.

Hyperlinks to headings are fairly strong. If you edit headings, your links still tend to connect. Links to bookmarks break easily if you edit the bookmark text.

TABLE OF CONTENTS

Use **Table of Contents** to make a List of Choices. Anyone who makes eBooks will generally be familiar with table of contents or TOC. Word makes this really easy. Okay, not that easy – for some reason they have parked it under the references tab, which does not seem logical to me. You'll get a couple of choices setting up your table of contents. Remember to uncheck page numbers. Page numbers don't exist in eBooks, only locations.

When you've made your TOC you should also *bookmark the heading as TOC*. That way Amazon recognizes it as a TOC and lists it in your Kindle's menu. This is vital. Don't miss this step.

In interactive fiction, the TOC is a great tool of communication between you and the reader. Readers don't want to wade through pages and pages of content to try a different branch. Giving your readers a List of Choices helps them return.

TYPE SIZE AND FONTS

We don't use anything more than a 2 point difference inside our books. We use 12 point for the body text (normal) and 14 point for the largest headings. Readers set their own font size and preferred font on eReaders – you are really only setting size variance. If you keep the variance minimal, it will work more consistently across different devices. On the cross trainer at the gym I read in large print mode so I don't have to wear my glasses. Over-designed eBooks often look terrible and put me off buying more from that author.

PAGE BREAKS

You don't have control of where page breaks will occur. You should imagine your eBook as flowing text. Some interactive books insert a page break before and after a choice. We don't like the look of page breaks before a choice because this can result in large gaps that disrupt reading. We insert page breaks after choices to clearly signal the end of sections. An efficient way to do this is to insert the page break into your heading style. Be consistent with whatever you do. The more organized you are about your layout and layout conventions, the easier it will be to modify them later.

Moving and editing sections

Move sections around using the navigation pane. This is much less error-prone than using copy and paste to move big chunks of text. Click on a section in the navigation pane and then drag it to where you want it. (Sorry, this doesn't work in earlier versions of Word.) When you are writing sections of a story, you can 'demote' headings to sub-headings for a tranche of story and then 'promote' them. Always test your links after moving them.

Marketing

THE MARKET

- Tablet use in schools is on the rise with great programs like Mathletics and Khan Academy using electronic devices.

- Cheaper smart phones and tablets mean children are being gifted secondhand devices from parents. Some are given new devices directly. Kids are reading using tablets, Kindle devices and phones.

- There is still some wariness from parents that kids shouldn't read on electronic devices. Some parents encourage Kindles over tablets, because kids can't play games or access the web.

- Paper books? Don't let the limitations of paper limit what you can do with eBooks. For a long time we didn't make paper books. We do make paper books now, and they do sell, but we simplify our paper books and omit our more link-heavy stories (Sorcerers Maze mini-series) – design for eBooks first.

- Since first publishing in 2012, I've seen a steady increase in interactive fiction books online. Poor quality books soon sink to the bottom of the pile.

- In August of 2016, I estimated that there were 3000 new books launching on Amazon every day. Of those, nearly ten percent were kids' books. That's the size of our competition.

- Most independent authors only ever produce one book and they don't sell many copies. It's easy to see why. To get noticed you need quality and volume in the same genre. When you finish a great book, what do you usually do? I usually look for another book by the same author. To be successful you need to write more than one book and remember this: Writing is a long game.

YOUR BRAND

If you are considering more than one work of interactive fiction, you will want to think about your brand from the beginning. Here are some pointers to making your work recognizable and cohesive:

- Consider a series name or a repeating theme in your titles. Do not use well-known interactive fiction series names, even in passing, as many of these are trademarked and some of these firms will track you down and threaten litigation.
- Think about your cover design. Choose something that has scope for variety but strong elements you can repeat. If you choose some repeatable elements, make sure you hold the rights – not your designer.
- Consider a standard opening line or setup for your brand.
- Decide if you will let other authors contribute to the series and how you will manage this.
- Consider writing *You Say Which Way* for The Fairytale Factory!

We took our time developing the *You Say Which Way* brand. We wanted something that really 'said what was in the tin.' We wanted something memorable and unique. We had published more than four books and had compiled our first box set before we settled on *You Say Which Way*. The beauty of publishing online is it allows you to develop as you go. Once we had the *You Say Which Way* brand name, we could go back and add it to the earlier books.

An alternative approach to a series title is to follow a convention in your title. Gerry Gaston starts each of his titles with the same three words: *Quest for the Dragon's Treasure, Quest for the Pirate Treasure* etc.

In designing the *You Say Which Way* covers, I took my inspiration from a postage stamp. I wanted something recognizable when it was reduced to a small size. I noticed many book covers became indistinguishable when they were the size of a stamp – yet online this is typically how they are presented. I used a frame that could be repeated across genres and then mocked up a few concepts to ensure I could achieve something recognizable, but also add variety.

The design deliberately doesn't give the author name prominence. I wanted the brand to give the promise of delivering the same reader experience, regardless of the author. I had an inkling that I might collaborate with other authors or publish other writers. I wanted everyone's name on the work, but I wanted the reader to understand they would be getting the same style and quality regardless of the main author (see the cover examples on the back cover of this book).

When adults reminisce about reading interactive fiction, they often remember the standard introductions the 1980s books typically had. Your introduction can be a fun feature of your brand. It also serves as an early warning to unsuspecting readers and buyers that this is an interactive book. People don't always react well to surprises, and you don't want a lack of warning to trigger a poor review.

We've developed and refined a standard introduction over time. I'm always tinkering with this. I don't think I've cracked the perfect intro yet, but I do want to convey that the book is interactive, that you say which way, and that you may not survive BUT you can try again.

Here is my draft intro from *The Magician's Cat* – my work in purrrrrrogress.

This is a book which doesn't play straight. The magician's house is like that too – things move around. If you're the sort of person who needs predictability, then pick up another book, curl up and enjoy it. This book won't mind.

But, if you're willing to wing it:

Go straight to the story

Or: If you need more clues to help you move around, then go here:

Learn more about navigating this story on your device

Note that I offer some instruction on how to navigate the story.

Some eReaders are a bit clunky, and back in 2012 (so long ago now!) we thought instruction was required. We have never had a complaint that people can't use hyperlinks, so we may drop this one day.

MULTIPLE AUTHORS

Children's literature has a great tradition of series that are produced by multiple authors. The *Warrior Cats* series uses the pseudonym Erin Hunter for a collective of six writers. The *Nancy Drew* series began in 1930 and new material is still coming out under the brand name. It is almost impossible to compile a full list of the number of authors who have written for the character. Trixie Belden is another plucky girl detective penned by multiple authors.

One of the advantages of having multiple authors write for a series is the ability to produce volume. A more important advantage we have recognized is that the authors can learn from one another. I started off by critiquing the work of the 1980s and trying to develop work that suited a Kindle reader this century. Blair Polly brought a strong interest in the incorporation of non-fiction and puzzles to the books. Peter Friend really pushed the boundaries of second person characters for us, and Eileen Mueller is a master of action prose and humor. Unlike a lot of publishing houses where writers are unaware of each other's work, we read and critique each other and the stories are better for it.

There are advantages and disadvantages of publishing under multiple author names on Amazon. The Amazon algorithm links tightly by category, age range (in the case of children's books) and author. The fantastic Amazon marketing machine may not understand that your books are 'like each other' even if they have the same series name. Numbering your series will help Amazon understand they are linked. Numbering a series may put readers off reading a title they discover because they think they need to read the series in order. Luckily, you can experiment and find out what works best for you.

SERIES

It's a no-brainer to have a series name if you publish on Amazon, because it's one of the ways Amazon figures out that the books are like each other.

One point in favor of a numbered series is the series banner which Amazon gives some books at its own discretion. Books which clearly follow on from each other are entitled to the banner. Books which share a brand name but don't follow on from each other are not always permitted a series banner.

If you are publishing under different author names, you will need a series to tie the work together.

A FEW NOTES ABOUT EREADING AND EBOOKS

Hopefully you've bought some eBooks and gleaned a bit about the market as a reader. If you haven't bought books online, you should. In particular I'd encourage you to read with a Kindle and a tablet if you haven't already.

I'm continuously intrigued by the slightly different experience of eReading. Digital reading already has a lot of choice in it. Kids reading on a tablet can look up words they don't understand with a built-in dictionary. (Adults can too.) So, although you don't want to make your reader feel stupid and turn away from your story, you can sometimes get away with being a bit more technical with your language where it's appropriate.

Readers' habits vary. When I'm at the bus stop in the morning, I bring up the latest book I'm reading on my phone. I mainly read on my iPad at home. If I'm connected to the internet, the Kindle app will ask me if I want to sync to the furthest place I've read on any device. I don't always leap to where I was last night on my iPad, sometimes I like to re-read on my commute. Sometimes my mother and I are reading the same book at the same time, so I'll just page forward. Your Kindle account can be fed to eight reading devices, which is great for families. Sometimes I'll go find a bookmark and re-read a section I liked. I also bookmark recipes in books! Barbara Kingsolver's excellent non-fiction account of eating seasonally (*Animal, Vegetable, Miracle: Our Year of Seasonal Eating*) is peppered with great recipes. If I was her publisher I would have created a quick table of links to the recipes. No matter, bookmarks to the rescue!

Another thing I do, when I'm reading great or insightful writing, is use the tablet's inbuilt camera to photograph pages I like. As I read through Stephen King's *On Writing*, I was constantly exclaiming 'Yes!' as he dropped one truth after another for me. I'd be paging back and bookmarking like crazy and then I thought: why not make a quick album of the parts that I love? So I now have a Stephen King *On*

Writing highlights photo album. I doubt it's an original idea. This works great for recipes too!

It isn't unusual for writers to make Pinterest boards these days as they work on their first drafts. It's a great way to build an idea of your world and get fresh ideas from pictures you collect. I have Pinterest boards for most of my books, and I've seen fans put together homage boards for favorite series. (Just search *Game of Thrones*, fairytales, or Nancy Drew in Pinterest and you'll get the picture!)

If you haven't noticed, I absolutely love eReading and chuckle at people who say, "I've never read an eBook." Poor things. There's nothing better than having a library in a wafer. My mother is 81 this year and she loves her Kindle. She's rereading Dickens and Shakespeare and many more. "And look how light it is," she laughs. "You'd have thought Shakespeare would have weighed it down."

It's not just the classics people tote around. I regularly go to meetings in which people arrive with tablets, pull up technical documents on the fly, and get more done than we did in the old paper days.

And while I'm on the topic of eBooks, I will mention the impact that web reading is having on our navigation of written material. We nearly all google these days. It's a verb. We navigate with language, not a compass. The web is a giant interactive collection of words and pictures, and it's sometimes strange to me that the classical form of the story has stayed so stoically linear.

If you get a chance, take a look at a website called Arts and Letters Daily. It might not be your cup of tea, but pause and look at how it is structured. Its layout has remained the same since it started. Four columns wide, like a newspaper, with a heading and a paragraph acting as a top-level, patchwork quilt of hooks. Simple, yet so effective. To me, this is a form of interactive fiction.

So:

- reading, in general, is becoming more interactive.
- readers can cope with a lot more interactivity these days, because it is part of their general online experience, and
- please don't try to write interactive fiction without first reading quite a few eBooks yourself.

A FEW NOTES ABOUT AMAZON

There are plenty of books about publishing on Amazon. Nearly all the advice you can buy about Amazon is available free on the web. There isn't much about interactive fiction for kids, though, so that's what this section is about.

Good news! Amazon has an interactive fiction category. In fact it has a couple. It has one in its kids' section as well as one for adults. That means people can actually search for interactive fiction and, if they buy interactive fiction, Amazon will recognize this and suggest more of it to the customer. Interactive fiction is part of Amazon's recognition system. It ranks the top 100 kids' interactive fiction books. I love it when our books are in the top 20 because that means Amazon is more likely to be spamming people about them.

If you publish on Amazon, you'll join over 6 million titles. The number is growing every day. If your work is good, it still may not float to the top. You should write interactive fiction (or whatever you write) because you enjoy it. Don't write to get rich. Almost nobody does.

General notes writing for children

- You don't only have a contract with the reader to uphold, you have a contract with a parent.
- Orphan your child – fiction for young people works best when they are autonomous.
- Give your main character a clear desire or a problem to solve.
- Don't describe detailed violence and question the need for violent content.
- No prejudice. Leave sexism and racism at the door.
- Avoid negative stereotypes e.g. male doctors, female characters doing all the cooking, people of color 'saved' by Europeans.
- Encourage diversity in interesting ways.
- Kids like reading about characters slightly older than themselves – growing up is part of the aspirational reader experience.
- Kids' stories are often more explicit about what the character wants.
- Kids don't usually have all the facts, so provide characters who question and ways to get answers.
- The plot should be kid-driven. Kids should solve the problem themselves or achieve their goal through their own ingenuity – although they can get help on the way.

Many musicals and animated stories start with an "I wish" song. Disney's *Snow White* starts with a song at the wishing well literally singing "I'm wishing…" for her prince.

In *Into the Woods* all the characters are seen in a song that expresses their greatest desire – to go to the festival, to have a cow, to have a child, etc. The rest of the story is a pathway to achieving those desires – with a few roadblocks in the way.

Here are some examples of roadblocks:
- a nemesis who wants to thwart them or take their stuff
- a final show-down with that nemesis
- people who need to be helped
- a fairy godmother character who provides skills or tools
- a sidekick to keep them company and provide help along the way
- a perilous journey to get to a destination (e.g. *Lord of the Rings*)
- danger
- characters preventing them from making progress
- a skill they're lacking that they need to fulfill their deepest desire
- their own weakness

How to improve your writing

Obviously, **read a lot**. Read critically. Read widely. Most formal courses will tell you to keep a reading diary to gain a critical awareness of what you're reading.

Questioning the techniques used by other writers helps you to emulate things that work well. Here are some useful questions:

- Why did the author start the story there? Were there other places the story could have begun?

- How about the ending – if you are lucky enough to have kept a reader all the way through a story, the ending is the point at which things get wrapped up and wound down. New writers often skid to the end with a bang while more seasoned writers learn the fine art of winding down. In interactive fiction, endings tend to be short but you still want to provide a wind-down as well as resolution.

- Why and how did we empathize with the characters? How did the characters develop?

- What elements of the story made you keep reading?

- How did you feel ethically about the story? What would you do differently?

- What were your favorite scenes? Why?

- What were your favorite plot twists?

- What surprised you about the book? Did you like those surprises?

- How did the author use imagery, voice, setting?

- What was the key conflict/drama in the book? How was this developed?

If you want to write interactive fiction then **read interactive fiction** – especially modern interactive fiction. Read the stuff people are writing for adults. Read spooky books, read the puzzle-based books, look at the online material people don't see as interactive fiction and think about what the reader contract is. How do you know how to navigate it? What conventions and rules are the writer using? How would you improve the book?

Reading short stories for younger readers will improve your critical awareness of storytelling for middle-grade readers. Paul Jennings is a particular favorite of mine. *Zombies vs Unicorns* is a popular short story collection for a slightly older age group (12-15 years). Reading and comparing the text of these stories will help you land the middle-grade pitch.

Show your work to other people. Ask them how you could improve it and welcome their suggestions. You might not always agree, but you will always learn something.

Get a great editor. Sub your work everywhere. There is nothing wrong with self-publishing, just don't do it too early and don't slow down and spend all your precious time marketing your first work. Move on and write better stories. The more you write, the better you'll get.

Start or join a crit group. Get used to discussing writing with others and giving and receiving critical feedback. Try to get people into your group who have different backgrounds, are passionate about their writing (they aren't just there for the snacks and socializing) and have come from different writing schools.

Lastly, write. **Keep writing** and let yourself fall in love with your projects. Know that if you have a feedback loop (crit group, editors, beta readers and the gift of time to go back and look at your work) you'll get better. Don't expect perfection but aim for the highest quality you can achieve. Read. Write and Repeat.

Useful links and references

Carle, E. *The Very Hungry Caterpillar,* World Publishing Company, 1969

Diego Arandojo loved interactive fiction so much he created a musical tribute. This provides quick insight of the impact of interactive fiction on kids who don't normally feature in traditional books. www.menwhostareatbooks.co.uk/index.php/nathan-penlington-interviews-diego-arandojo-choose-your-own-adventure/

Edward Packard interview online: google: choosing-adventure-the-edward-packard-interview-part-i/

Emily Short's excellent blog on all things Interactive Fiction: emshort.wordpress.com/

Four More You Say Which Way Adventures, Friend, P., Mueller, E., Polly, B. and Potter, DM. Fairytale Factory, 2015. Full disclosure: I've got a story in this collection. There are four authors in this collection to give you a feel for different second person writing styles.

Jorge Luis Borges 1941 story The Garden of Forking Paths is commonly referred to as the inspiration of interactive fiction. Read a summary of the story on wikipedia.

King, S. *On Writing – A Memoir of the Craft*, Pocket Books, 2001. Not at all about interactive fiction but a great read for any writer.

Kingsolver, B. *Animal, Vegetable, Miracle: Our Year of Seasonal Eating*, Faber & Faber, 2010.

Matt Chat You Tube interview with Ray (RM) Montgomery January 2010: Google: matt+chat+Montgomery+youtube

Montfort, N. *Twisty Little Passages: An Approach to Interactive Fiction* (MIT Press), 2005

Podcast: Remembering RA Montgomery digital.vpr.net/post/remembering-ra-montgomery-who-helped-create-choose-your-own-adventure-books#stream/0

Podcast: We Tell Stories: Adrian Hon on video game and storytelling development   www.gdcvault.com/play/77/We-Tell-Stories-A-New

Schannep, James, *Click Your Poison* series 2013 onwards. James writes interactive fiction for grown-ups. It's great to read something pitched at your own reading level and contemplate your own reading experience.

Useful online tools

I have no commercial interest in any of these tools, they are just things I use regularly that get the job done.

Smarturl is a good free tool to create one universal link to use in blogs, on social media and websites. The link will take potential customers to their closest Amazon store. At the time of writing, the links also worked within books, as direct Amazon links have a habit of being blocked by Apple. Google: smarturl

GetBookReport gives you trends about your books (when you have lots of books) and its free if you earn less than US$1000 per month. So that's *most* Indie authors. www.getbookreport.com/

The **kindlepreneur** has a couple of tools I like. This first one is really cool. You put in your blurb text and it crafts the html to make it look as nice as a blurb can be. You still have to write a good blurb though! kindlepreneur.com/amazon-book-description-generator/

This second kindlepreneur tool gives you an estimate of the daily sales for a book if you put in its rank. It's probably good to recall the Desiderata when you use this tool: "If you compare yourself with others, you may become vain or bitter, for always there will be greater and lesser persons than yourself." kindlepreneur.com/amazon-kdp-sales-rank-calculator/

Yasiv allows you to see richer detail about the buying habits of your customers (or another book you are researching). This is great for understanding marketing connections and advertising. www.yasiv.com

About the Author

Deb Potter is an author of 'You Say Which Way' books and owner of the publishing company, The Fairytale Factory.

She lives in New Zealand, which is just above Antarctica – but isn't quite as cold. Her adolescence saw her produce a lot of terrible poetry. She also found time to write plays, one of which won her a place at the first international young playwright's conference.

Deb started her working life as a reporter, which gave her the habit of asking questions, and she's never stopped since then.

At university, Deb first studied social and public policy and research techniques. Throughout her studies she worked part-time at Wellington Public Library, where she rediscovered children's books.

Deb has a certificate in Children's Literature from Christchurch College of Education – now part of Canterbury University. The papers were mainly aimed at teachers and librarians – the people who would have the power to choose which books kids got access to.

Her long career in statistics involved the creation of complex social surveys and gave her a great affinity for flow charts. Deb continued to write and published her first interactive story in 2012. The following year she did a full-time Masters in Creative Writing while also working 30 hours a week and caring for her two kids. It was a busy year that helped her think about what she most wanted to do in her life.

Today she works 'democratizing data' four days a week, and runs The Fairytale Factory the rest of the time, writing and editing interactive fiction.

What did you think?

How did I do? Do you have a better understanding of interactive fiction? Do you feel like giving it a go? You can send unanswered questions and general comments for improvement via the *You Say Which Way* website www.YouSayWhichWay.com. I'll respond to you personally and update this manual for future readers. Please let other potential readers know what you think with a review.

May your life be filled with wonderful choices!

Deb (DM) Potter

YouSayWhichWay.com